Cute Clothes

for the Crafty Fashionista

by Tina Dybvik

CAPSTONE PRESS

a capstone imprint

Snap Books are published by Capstone Press,
1710 Roe Crest Drive, North Mankato, Minnesota 56003.
www.capstonepub.com

Books published by Capstone Press are manufactured with paper
containing at least 10 percent post-consumer waste.

Library of Congress Cataloging-in-Publication Data

Dybvik, Tina.
Cute clothes for the crafty fashionista / by Tina Dybvik.
      p. cm. — (Snap books. Fashion craft studio)
Summary: "Step-by-step instructions for T-shirts, jeans, skirts, and other clothing crafts made from
repurposed materials"—Provided by publisher.
ISBN 978-1-4296-6553-7 (library binding)
1. Clothing and dress—Remaking—Juvenile literature. I. Title. II. Series.

TT550.D93 2012
646.34—dc22   2011002453

Editor: Mari Bolte
Designer: Heidi Thompson
Photo Stylist: Sarah Schuette
Project Production: Marcy Morin
Production Specialist: Laura Manthe

Photo Credits:
all photos by Capstone Studio/Karen Dubke, Shutterstock/vienkat

Capstone would like to thank Rosanne Guararra for her help in producing the projects in this book.

Printed in the United States of America in North Mankato, Minnesota.
032012   006682R

Table of

Do-it-Yourself Style

Clean out your closet and redefine your style! Whether your image is preppy, punk, or posh, there's a low-cost way to make a fashion statement. You can turn last season's standbys into this season's trends—but ask before you alter!

Armed with some old clothes and a few supplies, you'll be ready to change up your closet! Surprise your family, friends, and yourself with these DIY designs.

Where to Begin?

Most of the materials you'll need are within reach. Check your closet to find shirts, hats, and pants that fit your body but not your style. If you don't see what you need, check secondhand thrift shops or craft and fabric stores. With a just few hours and some patience, you can become your own fashion designer.

The directions in this book are only ideas. You might not have the same shirts, fabric, trim, or decorations as shown. Don't worry about it! Let your inner designer create one-of-a-kind clothes your friends will envy!

1. sleeve hem
2. sleeve seam
3. collar
4. shoulder seam
5. underarm seam
6. side seam
7. bottom hem

It's easy to change measurements to metric! Just use this chart.

To change	into	multiply by
inches	centimeters	2.54
inches	millimeters	25.4
feet	meters	.305
yards	meters	.914

Fem **Fedora**

Add a feminine touch to a classic fedora hat. Use ribbons in complementary colors and flair that fits your style. Pair your hat with a cute outfit and become a runway star in your own fashion world. Are you ready for your close-up?

You Will Need:

measuring tape
fedora hat
scissors
thick ribbon, at least 1 inch wide
thinner ribbon, ½ to ¾ of
    an inch wide, in a
    contrasting color

hot glue
chain or necklace long
    enough to go around the
    fedora at least once
feather hat pin

Step one:
Measure the length around the crown of the fedora.

Step two:
Cut both ribbons to measured length.

Tip: Don't feel tied down to ribbons. Strips of fabric from old shirts, dresses, ties, and even old belts could be used.

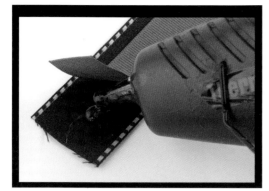

 **Step three:**
Center the thinner ribbon on top of the thicker ribbon. Glue in place. Let glue dry completely.

 **Step four:**
Pull the brim of the hat down to make gluing easier. Glue the layered ribbons onto the hat. Let dry completely.

 **Step five:**
Loop the chain around the hat, gluing along the way. Reposition the hat's brim.

 **Step six:**
Pin the feather to the hat.

complementary—things that look good together

Fringed 'n Flirty Scarf

Wrap yourself in a trendy patterned scarf in hip, hot colors that flatter all year round. The latest shades will pop against last season's shirts and jackets. Have friends choose the colors that are best on you. Wear the scarf loose, or twist it tight to warm up yourself and your look.

You Will Need:

one cotton T-shirt
scissors
paintbrush
glitter fabric paint
beads

Step one:
Lay T-shirt flat on work surface.

Step two:
Cut T-shirt straight across, from underarm seam to underarm seam. Discard the top part of the shirt.

Step three:
Paint the bottom inch of the shirt. Allow paint to dry.

Step four:
From the bottom of the shirt, make straight cuts halfway up the T-shirt. The cuts should be about ½-inch wide.

Step five:
Continue making cuts across the entire shirt.

Step six:
Slip beads onto random pieces of fringe. Tie a double knot to keep beads in place.

seam—a line of sewing that joins two pieces of cloth

Denim and Lace

Vintage tradition is always in style. Decorate your denim with a lacy trim. Use lace to patch holes in your pants. The contrast is sweet and simple. Your friends will beg to know where your lacy jeans came from!

You Will Need:

pair of denim jeans
pieces of lace fabric
   in various sizes
measuring tape or ruler

scissors
iron
fabric glue
jewels

Step one:

Decide what parts of your jeans should be covered in lace. Select appropriate-sized pieces of lace for each area. Large pieces of lace will be best for covering holes or legs. Small pieces will be better for trim.

Step two:

Cut lace to fit.

Step three:

With an adult's help, wash and iron the lace.

vintage—from the past

Step four:

Use fabric glue around the edges of the lace. Press the lace onto jeans. Let dry.

Step five:

Add jewels or other embellishments to lace for some sparkle 'n shine.

Tip: If you can't find a lace pattern you like, look for lace appliqués. Lace and appliqués can be found at craft, fabric, and thrift stores. See pages 16–17 for instructions on using appliqués.

appliqué—a cutout decoration fastened to a larger piece of cloth

embellishment—a decoration that adds detail to something

Ribbons and Rings

Where will waistlines be this year? Will high, empire-waisted shirts be in? Or will the shirt waists be low on the hips? It's an ever-changing trend. This ribbon belt will help you follow the fashion. Cinch your belt low with your favorite jeans or up high with a tee.

You Will Need:

measuring tape
scissors
1- to 2-inch-wide heavy,
   stiff ribbon
rhinestone or sequin trim
needle and thread
two 2-inch metal D-rings

Step one:

Decide where on your body you want to wear the ribbon. Measure and cut enough ribbon and trim to go around your waist about one and a half times.

Step two:

Use the needle and thread to sew the trim to the ribbon.

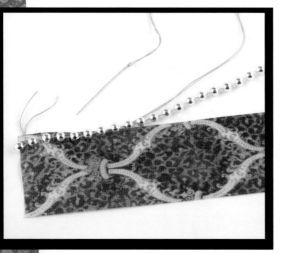

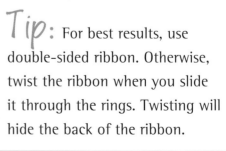

Tip: For best results, use double-sided ribbon. Otherwise, twist the ribbon when you slide it through the rings. Twisting will hide the back of the ribbon.

Step three:
Fold and sew the ends of the ribbon to create a hem.

Step four:
Slide the other end of the ribbon through the D-rings. Pull the ribbon back through the top ring. Sew the ribbon to the rings. Cinch to fit.

Sewing by Hand:
Slide the thread through the eye of the needle. Tie the end of the thread into a knot. Poke the needle through the underside of the fabric. Pull the thread through the fabric to knotted end. Poke your needle back through the fabric and up again to make a stitch.

Continue weaving the needle in and out of the fabric, making small stitches in a straight line. When you are finished sewing, make a loose stitch. Thread the needle through the loop and pull tight. Cut off remaining thread.

hem—the border of an article of clothing

Tee-Cycling

This crossover piece is half scarf, half necklace, and all recycled. Turn a plain old tee into an eye-catching accessory that can be worn anywhere you want to go.

You Will Need:

two soft cotton T-shirts
scissors
ruler
pencil
an old necklace

Step one:

Lay T-shirts on your work surface. Cut off the hem of each shirt.

Step two:

Use ruler to measure straight, horizontal lines across the bottom of the shirts every ½ inch. Use pencil to mark lines.

Step three:

Cut horizontally across the pencil lines to make fabric loops. Cut at least 12 loops.

Step four:

Hold both seams of the loops. Stretch loops until they curl into strands.

Step five:

Stack the strands and line up all the seams.

Step six:

Make a figure-8 twist with the strands. Bring the seams together to form a circle.

Step seven:

Unhook the necklace and wrap it around the strands to hide the seams. Hook the ends of the necklace back together. Your scarf is ready to wear!

Tip: Go beyond a simple neck warmer. Accessorize by wrapping your new scarf around your ankle or wrist. Or try wearing it in your hair as a headband.

Stylin' **Shorts**

Seasons and styles change, but there's always a need for shorts. Turn old castoffs into colorful cutoffs with these soft appliqué patches. Scour your closet for fabric remnants to give your patches a personal touch.

You Will Need:

an old pair of jeans

ruler

scissors

needle and thread (optional)

empty cereal box

iron-on adhesive paper

old T-shirts, scarves, dresses,
    or other fabric remnants

iron

Step one:

Lay jeans flat. Decide how short
or as long you want them to be.

Step two:

Cut jeans 4 inches below
your desired length.

Step three:

Fold the bottoms of the jeans
up to create cuffs. Sew cuffs,
if desired.

Step four:

Draw and cut out shapes on the cereal box. Make your shapes three different sizes.

Step five:

Trace shapes onto the adhesive paper. Make sure they're facing the opposite way you want your patches to face. Cut your new adhesive shapes out.

Step six:

Lay adhesive shapes on the back of cotton remnants. Follow the instructions on the adhesive paper package. Have an adult help you iron the shapes onto the remnants.

Step seven:

Cut out your adhesive shapes from the remnants.

Step eight:

With an adult's help, iron adhesive shapes onto shorts.

Backward **Batik**

The art of wax dying known as batik dates back more than 2,000 years. People are still inspired by these dyed patterns. But batik is a difficult technique. Make things easy with everyday household items. Use your skills to create a clever reversed batik pattern. Turn plain tees into tops that make a lasting impression.

You Will Need:

dark cotton shirt
newspaper
flattened cereal box, empty
lace fabric doilies
all-purpose cleaning spray
    with bleach
aluminum foil
heavy book or other weight

 **Step one:**
Lay the shirt front side up on top of a work surface covered with newspaper.

Tip: Stray drops of cleaning spray will make permanent stains, so wear old clothes. Be sure to do this project in an open area, and have an adult nearby to help. If you have delicate skin, wear rubber gloves for protection.

 **Step two:**
Lay cereal box inside shirt. The box will protect the back of the shirt.

technique—a method or a way of doing something that requires skill

 **Step three:**
Plan your design by laying doilies on top of the shirt.

 **Step four:**
Have an adult carefully spray cleaning liquid over the doilies. Spritz lightly rather than using a heavy spray. For even coverage, hold the spray bottle at least 1 foot above the shirt.

 **Step five:**
Use enough aluminum foil to completely cover the doilies. Weigh down doilies with a heavy book or weight.

 **Step six:**
Let the shirt rest for at least 30 minutes. Remove the weight, foil, and doilies. Be careful not to let doiles touch any other fabric. Wash or discard doilies immediately.

 **Step seven:**
Wash the shirt before wearing.

19

Beautiful Beanie

There's no wrong way to craft this cap. It will set off your face in a simple yet stunning way. Sport it while strolling down the street or wear it while cheering on your favorite team.

You Will Need:

seam ripper
baseball cap
fabric glue
fabric scraps (at least ½ yard
    to cover entire hat)
jewels
embellishments

Step one:
Use the seam ripper to open the seams on the hat's brim. Remove the visor from the hat.

Tip: Use the seam ripper to distress the cap by adding a tiny rip or two.

Step two:
The seams that connect the visor to the hat also connect the hat's liner. Use glue to keep the liner in place.

Step three:

Glue the fabric scraps to the hat.

Step four:

Use smaller pieces of fabric to cover any uneven areas, wrinkled fabric, or loose edges. Let dry.

Step five:

Glue jewels and embellishments onto the hat. Let dry.

distress—a technique that makes new clothes look old

Rosettes or Ruffles?

These short 'n sporty jackets go by many names including shrugs, boleros, and wraps. Use yours to cover up on a cool night or dress down your eveningwear to go out with friends.

You Will Need:

long-sleeved T-shirt

scissors

yard stick or straight edge

chalk

scissors

needle and thread

Step one:

Lay the shirt flat on your work surface. Use the scissors to remove the neckline. Remove the hem from both sleeves.

Step two:

Put on the shirt. Decide how short you want your jacket to be. Mark the desired length with chalk while wearing the shirt. This line will be the midriff mark.

Step three:

Take off the shirt. Use the chalk to draw a line down the center of the T-shirt.

Step four:

Near the bottom of the shirt, measure 2 inches on both sides of the center line. Chalk two vertical lines from the T-shirt's hem to the midriff mark. These lines will become the ties for your jacket.

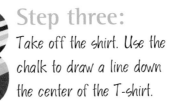

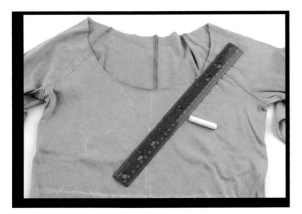

Step five:

At the top of the shirt, measure 3 inches down the center line. From this point, draw two chalk lines to either end of the shirt's neck hole, forming a triangle.

continue on next page

Step six:

Cut shirt in this order:
1. ties
2. midriff line (do not cut through the ties!)
3. center line
4. triangle

Step seven:

Fasten the ties. You're ready to wear your shirt in style!

To make the rosette(s):

Step one:

Use the leftover fabric to trace and cut five circles of varying sizes.

Step two:

Stack the circles by size with the smallest on top. Lay the circles on top of the shirt.

Step three:
Repeat steps 1 and 2 until you have enough rosettes to make a border.

Step four:
Sew rosette to jacket with three to four stitches in the flower's center. This will create the petals and puckers of the flower.

Variation:
- Use another shirt or a different fabric color to really make the rosettes pop.

Skirting the Issue

You'll glide down the runway in a swirl of color. An old dress can become a swishy skirt with just a snip here and a stitch there. Use a bold print to keep the flounce factor high!

You Will Need:

high-waisted dress	scissors
straight pins	needle and thread
measuring stick	1-inch wide elastic
chalk	large safety pin

Step one:
Try on the dress and decide the perfect waist and hem height.

Step two:
Use a straight pin to mark the new waistline. Then take off the dress and turn it inside-out.

Step three:
Measure 3 inches above the pin. Use the chalk to mark your measurement all the way around the dress.

Step four:
Cut the dress on the chalk line and set aside the top.

Step five:
Fold the top of the skirt over at least 1 inch. Fold again, to form a casing.

Step six:
Use straight pins to hold the folds in place.

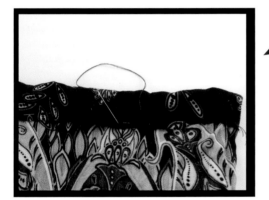

Step seven:
Use straight pins to hold the casing in place. Sew the bottom edge with a slip stitch.

Sewing the Slip Stitch:

Thread the needle, tie a knot, and secure it at the starting point. Take a tiny stitch (just a couple of threads) in the garment, and then slip the needle sideways through the folded edge for about ¼ inch.

Pull the needle and thread through the fold to tighten the stitch slightly (but not so tight it puckers.) Repeat stitches across the length of the waistband. Remember to hide your stitches and make them invisible.

continue on next page

Step eight:

Measure and cut the elastic to fit your waist. Fasten the safety pin to one end of the elastic.

Step nine:

Cut a small opening in the casing. Thread the elastic through the casing. Be careful not to let the other end of the elastic get pulled into the casing.

Step ten:

Once the elastic is threaded through, pin the two ends together.

Step eleven:

Try on your skirt to check the size. Be sure the elastic is snug. Add ¼ of an inch for overlap.

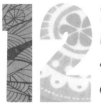

Step twelve:

Use the needle and thread to sew the elastic together and the ends of the folds shut. Turn the skirt right-side-out and wear with style!

✸ Variations:

- Turn the top of the dress into a matching headband or scarf.
- Use ribbon instead of elastic to make a drawstring skirt.

Tip: To keep the elastic from twisting, add a few extra stitches at the side seam casing.

Glossary

appliqué (a-pluh-KAY)—a cutout decoration fastened to a larger piece of cloth

complementary (KAHM-pluh-muhnt-uh-ree)—things that look good together

distress (di-STRES)—a technique that makes new clothes look old

embellishment (em-BELL-ish-mehnt)—a decoration that adds detail to something

hem (HEMM)—the border of an article of clothing made by folding the edge and sewing it down

remnant (REM-nehnt)—a small piece of something

seam (SEEM)—a line of sewing that joins two pieces of cloth

technique (tek-NEEK)—a method or a way of doing something that requires skill

vintage (VIN-tij)—from the past

Read **More**

Kelley, K. C. *Fashion Design Secrets.*
Reading Rocks! Mankato, Minn.: Child's
World, 2009.

Sirrine, Carol. *Cool Crafts with Old Jeans: Green
Projects for Resourceful Kids.* Green Crafts. Mankato,
Minn.: Capstone Press, 2010.

Torres, Laura. *Rock Your Wardrobe.* QEB Rock
Your ... Irvine, Calif.: QEB Pub., 2010.

Internet Sites

FactHound offers a safe, fun way to find
Internet sites related to this book. All of
the sites on FactHound have been researched
by our staff.

Here's all you do:

Visit *www.facthound.com*

Type in this code: 9781429665537

 Check out projects, games and lots more at
www.capstonekids.com

Index